PENGUIN BOOKS

Rilke: Selected Poems

Rainer Maria Rilke was born in Prague in 1875 and died in Valmont, Montreux, in 1926. Throughout his life he travelled restlessly around Europe, meeting Tolstoy in Russia (1900), working as 'secretary' to Rodin in Paris (1905–6), enjoying aristocratic hospitality (especially at Castle Duino, near Trieste, as guest of Marie von Thurn und Taxis, between 1910 and 1914), working as a clerk in Austria during the war, but finally settling at the Château de Muzot, Valais, after 1922.

The turning-points in his career are the *Neue Gedichte* ('New Poems') of 1907–8, together with the journal-novel of the same period, *Die Aufzeichnungen des Malte Laurids Brigge* (1910); and *Duineser Elegeien* and *Die Sonette an Orpheus* of 1922. His final interest was Paul Valéry whose poems, *Charmes*, he translated in 1925 and imitated in his own *Poèmes français*.

Selected Poems

RILKE

TRANSLATED WITH AN
INTRODUCTION BY
J. B. LEISHMAN

PENGUIN BOOKS

PENGUIN BOOKS

Published by the Penguin Group
Penguin Books Ltd, 80 Strand, London WC2R 0RL, England
Penguin Putnam Inc., 375 Hudson Street, New York, New York 10014, USA
Penguin Books Australia Ltd, Ringwood, Victoria, Australia
Penguin Books Canada Ltd, 10 Alcorn Avenue, Toronto, Ontario, Canada M4V 3B2
Penguin Books India (P) Ltd, 11 Community Centre, Panchsheel Park, New Delhi – 110 017, India
Penguin Books (NZ) Ltd, Cnr Rosedale and Airborne Roads, Albany, Auckland, New Zealand
Penguin Books (South Africa) (Pty) Ltd, 24 Sturdee Avenue, Rosebank 2196 South Africa

Penguin Books Ltd, Registered Offices: 80 Strand, London WC2R 0RL, England

www.penguin.com

This selection first published by Penguin Books 1964
(Poems chosen from *Poetry*, vol 2 of the *Selected Works*
published by the Hogarth Press 1960)
Reprinted in Penguin Classics 2000

2

Set in Garamond Monotype
Printed in England by Clays Ltd, St Ives plc

Contents

From THE SONNETS TO ORPHEUS: SECOND PART

From the UNCOLLECTED POEMS OF 1906 TO 1926

Introduction

Rainer Maria Rilke, the only surviving child of German-speaking and German-descended parents, was born in Prague on 4 December 1875. His father had been intended, like his two elder brothers, for the career of an officer in the Austrian army, but, after serving with distinction in the campaign against Italy in 1859, had been compelled to ask for a long leave of absence on grounds of ill-health, after which his prospects of promotion seemed so remote that he had resigned. He then became a railway official, but, although he achieved some success in this career, he remained until the end of his days a disappointed man, rather contemptuous of the bourgeois life he was forced to lead, and for many years found his one consolation in the hope that his son René (as he was originally called) would be able to obtain the commission he himself had been compelled to forgo. While Rilke's father appears to have been completely commonplace, his mother, though silly, snobbish, and full of a rather sentimental and superficial piety, had imagination of a kind and seems to have been something of a personality. Indeed, her son, to whom she bore a distinct facial resemblance, came in later years to regard her as a kind of caricature of himself. His birth had been preceded by that of a daughter, who had died in infancy, and his mother apparently tried to console herself for this loss by pretending, so long as she possibly could, that René was a girl. Until he was five years old he wore dresses and long curls and played with dolls, and even when these things had to go his only meetings with boys of his own age were on his birthdays.

When he was nine years old his parents separated, his father remaining in Prague while his mother went to live in Vienna; and partly, perhaps, because of this, partly because they could not afford to send him to a *gymnasium* (or, as the French would call it, a *lycée*), and partly because of the father's ambition that his son should become an officer, the precocious and so unwisely brought-up René was sent for five years (September 1886 to June 1891) to the Lower and Higher Military Schools of St Pölten and Mährisch-Weisskirchen, where all expenses were paid by the State. At these schools Rilke learnt little, made no friends, and suffered agonies of which he often spoke in later life. He was finally removed on the ground of continuous ill-health, and, after a year at the Commercial Academy in Linz, lived with his father in Prague and prepared himself, with the help of private tuition, for matriculation at the University. An uncle, a prosperous barrister, had proposed that he should succeed him in his practice and had offered to pay all the expenses of his education, but, although Rilke enrolled at the University as a student of law, he had already resolved to be a writer or nothing.

He wrote incessantly, both in prose and verse, did much reviewing, mixed in such literary circles as were to be found among the German minority in provincial and conservative Prague, and was full of ambitious projects for the foundation of literary journals and the production of plays. In later life he looked back with some shame and embarrassment on these activities, and declared that he only wrote and published so much because he wanted to prove to his unsympathetic and disapproving elders that he was capable of advancing himself in the career he had chosen. This early verse, which he wrote easily and with considerable virtuosity, is fluent, imitative (especially of Heine), and, for the most part, evocative of vaguely 'poetic' moods and attitudes; and it is fair to say of most of it (as was so falsely said by a notable Milton scholar of *Paradise Lost*) that the chief reason for reading it is to discover what was in the poet's mind when he wrote it. This applies not merely to the verse he wrote while still in Prague, but to the greater part of what he continued to write after he had left the University of Prague for that of Munich in 1896, and Munich for Berlin in October 1897. This is the period preceding the composition of the first part of *The Book of Hours,* which marks the beginning of his real importance as a poet.

His prose tales are much more objective and 'naturalistic', and often reveal, despite some grotesque lapses of taste, a remarkably keen eye for the individuality of people and things. To correct his overwhelming tendency to subjectivity, reverie, and rhapsody by developing his capacity for objectivity, to find more and more in outwardness, in actually existent things, 'objective correlatives' for his inwardness, and to ensure that every poem, however personal, should be not just an utterance but a 'thing made' (the original meaning of Greek *poiema*) became more and more the task of his life. In order that he might not be lamed by a continuous feeling of deprivation and resentment, he attempted to make a complete break with his early environment and to create for himself imaginatively a background and a childhood utterly different from his own. It might almost be said that the creation and maintenance of an ideal, poetic self became an important part of what he called his 'work', in which and for the sake of which he chiefly lived.

In Munich he was directed by Jakob Wassermann to the writings of the Danish poet and novelist Jens Peter Jacobsen, who, as he said later, strengthened his inner conviction 'that even for what is most delicate and inapprehensible within us Nature has sensuous equivalents that must be discoverable'; and in May 1897 he met Lou Andreas-Salomé, a woman considerably older than himself, who had been a close friend of Nietzsche's, and who now became a close friend and trusted counsellor to Rilke. She had been born in Russia, and encouraged Rilke, who moved to Berlin where she and her husband lived, to learn Russian and to begin a passionate study of Russian literature and history, and in the spring of 1899 he paid his first visit to Russia with her and her husband. Later he declared that he experienced there for the first time in his life something like a feeling of being at home and of belonging somewhere. In the following autumn, in a sudden and unexpected fit of continuous inspiration, he wrote *The Book of the Monastic Life*, the first part of what eventually became *The Book of Hours* (*Das Stundenbuch*), a cycle of sixty-seven short verse-meditations which are supposed to be those of a Russian monk, but in which Rilke's experience of Russia has coalesced with the scarcely less exhilarating and liberating experience of a long stay in Florence during the spring of 1898, when he had basked in what seemed to him the 'life-enhancing' this-worldliness of Italian Renaissance art. Art as a discovery and revelation of the mystery and wonder of life, poets, and painters as the true revealers and, in a sense, creators, of God – this was the conviction, or intuition, into which Rilke escaped from the narrow Catholicism of his early years, and this was the characteristically modified manner in which he accepted that Nietzschean life-worship, insistence on this-worldliness and rejection of other-worldliness, in which so many of his contemporaries found release. Nevertheless, although the 'prayers', as he called them, in Rilke's *Book of Hours* are not what many Christian readers might easily suppose them to be, and although what he is celebrating is, to a considerable extent, the creative energy, the intoxicating sense of power he is aware of in himself, it would be untrue to assert that the God he so frequently invokes has no relation to the God of religion and that the 'prayers' are addressed only to himself. What he called his 'work' came to mean for him more and more the experiencing and expression of 'reality', of intensity of 'being', and about his conception of reality and being, as about his dedicated search for them, there was something which, however much it may differ from true religion, can only be called religious.

From 7 May to 22 August 1900 he paid a second and much longer visit to Russia, this time with Lou Andreas-Salomé alone, and on his return he accepted an invitation to stay with a friend in the artists' colony of Worpswede, a remote heath village near Bremen. Here, in April 1901, he married the young sculptress Clara Westhoff, a pupil of Rodin's, settled down in a peasant's cottage in the neighbouring hamlet of Westerwede, and in September 1901 wrote *The Book of Pilgrimage*, the Second Part of his *Book of Hours*, full of his recent memories of Russia. A daughter was born, but it soon became clear to Rilke and his wife that it would be impossible, as they had hoped, to combine a dedicated pursuit of their respective arts with leading a simple life in their moorland cottage.

Sheer financial necessity would have compelled them to undertake all kinds of miscellaneous work which they would have regarded as a degradation; so they broke up their little household, entrusted their child to its maternal grandparents, and decided to pursue their careers separately and to meet as and when they could. Rilke (it was perhaps the most important event in his life) had received from a German publisher a commission to write a book on Rodin, and in August 1902 he departed for Paris, both in order to study the master's works and to meet the great man himself, for whom he had already, through his wife, conceived a boundless reverence and admiration, as one who had solved that problem of the opposition between art and life, of which Rilke was so continuously aware. Rodin would, he hoped, help him to achieve an ever more complete unification of his 'work' and his life.

Paris, with, it is true, many long absences, or, as Rilke often regarded them, 'truancies', remained his headquarters until the outbreak of war in 1914. His first letters from there are full of two things: admiration for Rodin and sensitive recoil from the miseries and horrors, the cruelty and indifference, of the city. In March 1903, unable to endure it any longer, he escaped for a month to Viareggio, and there wrote the third and last part of his *Book of Hours*, *The Book of Poverty and of Death*. The poems in all three parts are essentially outpourings, with a play of imagery and a rhythmical energy by which most readers who turn to them for the first time are irresistibly swept along. Rilke's attitude towards them remained ambiguous: on the one hand, he regarded them as improvizations rather than shapings or makings, written in a manner which he could have continued indefinitely; on the other hand, long after his conception of what a poem should be had become far more exacting, he often wished he could reachieve something like the inspired and exalted mood in and out of which they had been written. In July 1902, a month before his first arrival in Paris, he had published the first edition of his *Book of Images* (*Buch der Bilder*), containing poems written between 1898 and 1901, poems which might perhaps be described as neo-romantic, with, at their best, a peculiar combination of the descriptive, the evocative, and the symbolic, but still, for the most part, and in comparison with what he was soon to achieve, more or less obviously 'poetic' treatments of obviously 'poetic' subjects and moods.

He continued to write poems from time to time in this manner, and among the thirty-seven which he added to the second edition (1906) of the *Book of Images* are several which are very beautiful; but from the time of his first arrival in Paris, under the influence and example of Rodin, of French poets such as Baudelaire, and of French workmanliness and objectivity in general, he tried, at first occasionally and then more and more continuously and single-mindedly, to achieve something altogether different. The notion of a poet as one who just waited for the coming of poetic moods in which he could write 'poetically' about 'poetic' subjects became more and more distasteful to him. Could he not find some way of practising that precept which Rodin kept on repeating, *Il faut toujours travailler?* Could he not somehow, like a sculptor or a painter, set himself down day by day in front of his model and, without fussing about inspiration, simply get to work?

There is a story that one day he was trying to explain his problems and difficulties to Rodin, and that Rodin said to him: 'Why don't you just go and look at something – for example, at an animal in the *Jardin des Plantes*, and keep on looking at it till you're able to make a poem of it?'; that Rilke took this advice, and that the result was *The Panther*, the earliest of *New Poems* (*Neue Gedichte*), certainly written before September 1903, when it was published in a periodical, and possibly before the end of 1902. It was not, however, until the winter of 1905, the beginning of the period, lasting until May 1906, during which he lived in constant companionship with Rodin, that he attempted further examples of this new kind of short poem. In return for Rodin's hospitality he had offered to attend to the master's correspondence; this made enormous demands on his time, and the inevitable parting was precipitated by an unfortunate misunder-standing over a letter, to which Rilke had ventured to reply on his own initiative.

This eternal beginner, whom we so often find expecting or experiencing what he called a 'new beginning', now applied himself to the systematic and fairly continuous writing of that new kind of poem for which *The Panther* remained, as it were, his standard. The first part of *New Poems* was ready for the printer by the summer of 1907, and Rilke wrote of it to his wife: 'It's a book: *work*, the transition from inspiration that comes to that which is summoned and seized.' All the poems in the second part were written between the end of July 1907 and the middle of August 1908, and the volume, published in the follow-ing November, was dedicated 'A mon grand Ami Auguste Rodin'.

Many years later, writing to a friend about *New Poems*, Rilke declared that in them he had tried to give shape and form not to feelings, but to 'things I had felt'. In October 1907, three months after he had sent the manuscript of the first part to the printer, he was tremendously impressed by the exhibition of Cézanne's paintings at the Salon d'Automne, and for the next few weeks he wrote almost daily letters to his wife about Cézanne as a 'worker' and 'masterer of reality'. He professed to discover in these paintings what he called a turning-point, an immense progress in an altogether new kind of objectivity (*Sachlichkeit*), and he felt that he himself had reached such a turning-point, and had been instinctively striving towards a similar objectivity, in *New Poems*. There is indeed in these poems a wonderful balance between objectivity and subjectivity, inwardness and outwardness, French clarity and elegance and German *Innerlichkeit* (intensity). They are probably able to give more immediate pleasure to more lovers of poetry than any other portion of Rilke's work, and for that reason my selection from them is by far the largest in this book. Although they are re-creations, not just objective or naturalistic descriptions, the starting-point of almost every one of them is something that has (or had) a particular individual existence outside the poet, however much it may also have become something within him: a scene or incident from classical legend or the Bible; a representative figure from some period of European history or from modern life; a building, landscape, garden, or street-scene; an animal or a flower.

When Rilke came to arrange the poems for publication he adopted a roughly chronological sequence of subjects: in each part there is something like a historical panorama, occasionally interrupted by the appearance of landscapes, animals, or flowers, of what seemed to him most striking and significant in human civilization and achievement; evocations of early Greek antiquity are followed by scenes and incidents from the Old and New Testaments, and from these we proceed through the Middle Ages, the Renaissance, and the eighteenth century until we reach the modern world, which provides subjects for the majority of poems in each part. The two parts together contain nearly two hundred poems, and I can think of no other collection of short poems where the level of achievement is so consistently high. Every poem was intended to be, and usually is, as independent and self-sufficient as any painting, statue, building or other 'thing made'; while, though, some are purely descriptive and suggest nothing beyond themselves, others are in various ways representative or symbolic. Sometimes we just feel that they are in some way symbolic, although we cannot say precisely how, or of what; in others we can clearly feel that Rilke has found 'objective correlatives' for some of his own characteristic values and convictions.

For a time he continued to write poems of this kind and seems to have intended to complete yet a third Part of *New Poems*, but (and this is one of the most admirable things about him) he was never for long able to remain satisfied with any stage of achievement he had reached, however high. After his prolonged immersion in outwardness and objectivity, his awareness of the questionableness and problematicalness of the mere fact of individual existence returned with overwhelming force, and he gradually came to recognize that his next task must be the writing of a kind of poetry which, in a very special sense, would have to be lived before it could be written; for he must first achieve and then communicate some vision, some apprehension, of what might be called the value and destiny of the individual. What, in a world such as this, can finite beings like ourselves hope to achieve? What *are* we? What are we *for*? And he set himself the formidable task of formulating and finally (he hoped) answering these tremendous questions, not vaguely, abstractly, or discursively, but with a concentration, clarity, and concreteness not inferior to what he had achieved in *New Poems*.

The extreme 'difficulty' which is commonly ascribed to the *Duino Elegies* and to Rilke's later poetry in general is partly intrinsic and partly factitious – factitious, in the sense that it has been largely created by the preconceptions of his readers, by their attempts to discover in his poetry and to extract from it various abstract conceptions and philosophic ideas that were completely alien to him. For this poetry is in no sense the exposition of anything like a systematic philosophy, but an attempt to communicate, sometimes separately, sometimes in combination, some of Rilke's most intense, individual experiences of living and being, together with occasional hints and intuitions, reached in and through those experiences, into what might seem to be the true function and purpose in this world of the creature capable of receiving them. Here we encounter what for many readers (whether they recognize it or not) is the intrinsic difficulty: the fact that experiences which for Rilke are of central significance are for them only occasional, intermittent, or peripheral. Here, experiencing and reviewing life, is a very solitary man, one to whom institutions and organizations, which to most people mean so much, seem to mean almost nothing; one who is first and foremost a poet, and who tends to assess all other possible experiences in relation to those periods of creative perception and poetic creation in which he himself has experienced that 'completest possible inner intensity' which was his definition of 'being'. One, too, about whose dedicatedness to poetry and to his vocation as poet there is something almost religious, and to whom most human activities and preoccupations seem as trivial, superficial, and remote from 'man's chief end' as they might seem to one who had chosen the religious life.

Rejecting all conventional standards of value, he appeals to the imaginary figure of the Angel to evaluate the achievements of humanity. And yet, on the other hand, he is deeply aware of some fundamental conflict between the poetic vocation as he understands it, and life as it is generally understood – that 'normal' life which he himself is often tempted to envy, and sometimes, as it were, to escape into. In many of the poems written during those years of crisis 1910 to 1914 we find him torn between the claims of the super-human and the human, art and life, the Angel and the now longed-for, now rejected or renounced, Beloved. In that wonderful poem *The Spirit Ariel* (p 73) he has, at any rate until the closing lines, tried to identify himself with the figure of Prospero-Shakespeare saying farewell to art, and seems to have made of Ariel an embodiment of that something in life which he, as poet, has in some sense violated and perverted. On the other hand, in *The Stranger* (p 50, an earlier poem, of which, looking back from a later and distressful period, he said 'How well I knew what was required!') and in *The Great Night* (p 75) he has celebrated the final rewardingness of renunciation and endurance.

From October 1911 until May 1912 he stayed, mostly alone, at Schloss Duino, a castle on the Adriatic coast belonging to his friend Princess Marie von Thurn und Taxis, and there, after a long period of concentration and in a sudden fit of inspiration, he wrote in January and February 1912 the first two of what he eventually called the *Duino Elegies*. The beginnings of some of the other Elegies were also written during this winter in Duino, the Third was completed in Paris in 1913 and the Fourth was written in Munich in 1915 (Rilke had left Paris in July 1914 for a round of visits in Germany, and had been caught and kept there by the outbreak of war); but it was not until February 1922, at the little Château de Muzot, near Sierre, in the Swiss canton of Valais, where Rilke, who had left Germany for Switzerland in 1919, had at last found, through the generosity of a Swiss friend, the permanent refuge he had so long been seeking, that he was finally able, again in a sudden fit of inspiration following a long period of concentration, to complete the cycle of ten. And during this wonderful three weeks, shortly before and shortly after the completion of the *Duino Elegies*, he wrote the fifty-five entirely unexpected *Sonnets to Orpheus*.

Of the Elegies, I have here included the First, with its questions, and the Ninth, all of which, except the first six and the last three lines, was written at Muzot, and which is perhaps the fullest and most ambitious attempt at an answer. It certainly contains Rilke's fullest expression of a gradually and painfully achieved intuition into the inseparability of uniqueness and transience: into the central and tragic fact that individuals and individual experiences are unique because they are transient and transient because they are unique.

The completion of the *Duino Elegies* may be regarded as, in a sense, the end of something old; the *Sonnets to Orpheus*, together with many of the poems Rilke wrote during the remaining four years of his life, as the beginning of something new: a lifting, not indeed of the 'mystery' (to quote Wordsworth's famous line in the Tintern Abbey poem), but of the 'burden' of it; the achievement, as a reward for much patient endurance of silence, terror and perplexity, of the mood expressed in the beautiful poem beginning 'Meaningful word, "inclination"!' (p 81), the last of the numerous poems resulting from that great surge of creative energy in February 1922. On the fifth of December 1923 he copied it out for Katharina Kippenberg, the wife of his faithful friend and publisher, after receiving a birthday-telegram from her and her husband: he had, he said, discovered the lines a day or two before in a pocket-book, and it was his own wish for his birthday 'that this attitude (achieved here, at Muzot) which they express may remain ever more validly and enduringly mine'.

I have often been asked what the 'influence' of Rilke has been on German poetry, and the question has always depressed me. Attempts at anything like the direct imitation of a poet so intensely individual and original can never succeed, and readers who wish to see some of the results will find them exhibited in the final chapter of Mr H. M. Belmore's admirable book on *Rilke's Craftsmanship*. All that another poet might profitably try to imitate in Rilke would be his artistic integrity, his passion for perfection, and his willingness to remain a perpetual beginner. In November 1920, trying, in an earlier and temporary refuge, to achieve that degree of concentration which he later achieved at Muzot, he wrote to an intimate friend:

> Always at the commencement of work that first
> innocence must be re-achieved, you must return
> to that unsophisticated spot where the angel
> discovered you when he brought you the first
> binding message . . . If the angel deigns to
> come, it will be because you have convinced him,
> not with tears, but with your humble resolve to
> be always beginning: to be a beginner!

It remains for me to say a word or two about my methods of translation. While keeping as close as possible to the sense of the original, I have translated, not word for word, but phrase for phrase, and I have tried to preserve Rilke's metres, rhythms, rhyme-schemes, and syntax. Similes play a great part in his poetry, and perhaps no great poet has used the word 'like' so often; nevertheless, I am inclined to think that the innermost secret of his poetry is to be found not in its imagery, but in its syntax and rhythms. His long, winding sentences, full of subordinate clauses, questions, exclamations, parentheses, and participles and often extending throughout whole poems, communicate his attempts to analyse as accurately as possible, and with the maximum fullness compatible with the maximum concentration, just how particular 'things feel', and how they came to be what they were for him at particular moments. There is a continual outstretching and in-grasping, reflected in the contest between the metrical pattern and the rhythmical, or sentence, pattern, and it is this that gives to so many of his poems their characteristic-ally dramatic tension. It is largely according to his ability to reproduce this tension (which could not be communi-cated in prose) that a translation of Rilke will succeed or fail.

I hope I have also been able to reproduce something of the relationship between the language of his poetry and that of common speech, a relationship which even his most devoted German admirers have found formidably difficult to define. There is here a most subtle interplay between nature and artifice, formality and informality. We are perpetually surprised. Colloquial expressions are transfigured by the extreme precision and elegance of the verse-forms in which they appear, and wonderfully 'natural' speech-rhythms compel these strict verse-forms to behave in a manner of which we might have supposed them to be incapable. Here again there is tension, and all these tensions are a reflection of those within Rilke himself. 'We make out of the quarrel with others, rhetoric, but of the quarrel with ourselves, poetry', declared W. B. Yeats. In few great poets was the quarrel with themselves so continuous and so fruitful as in Rilke.

34

The day is coming when from God the Tree
a bough unlike that over Italy
in summer-ripe annunciance shall glisten;
here in a country where the people listen,
and everyone is solitary like me.

For only solitaries shall behold
the mysteries, and many of that mould
far more than any narrow one shall gain.
For each shall see a different God made plain,
till they acknowledge, near to crying,
that through their so diverse descrying,
through their affirming and denying,
unitingly diversifying,
one God rolls ever-flowingly.

This the conclusive hymn shall be
which then the seers will be singing:
Fruit out of God the Root is springing,
go, smash those bells that you were ringing;
we've reached that quieter season, bringing
the hour to full maturity.
Fruit out of God the Root is springing.
Be grave and see.

Childhood

The school's long stream of time and tediousness
winds slowly on, through torpor, through dismay.
O loneliness, O time that creeps away . . .
Then out at last: the streets ring loud and gay,
and in the big white squares the fountains play,
and in the parks the world seems measureless. –
And to pass through it all in children's dress,
with others, but quite otherwise than they: –
O wondrous time, O time that fleets away,
O loneliness!

And out into it all to gaze and gaze:
men, women, women, men in blacks and greys,
and children, brightly dressed, but differently;
and here a house, and there a dog, maybe,
and fear and trust changing in subtle ways: –
O grief uncaused, O dream, O dark amaze.
O still-unsounded sea!

And then with bat and ball and hoop to playing
in parks where the bright colours softly fade,
brushing against the grown-ups without staying
when ball or hoop their alien walks invade;
but when the twilight comes, with little, swaying
footsteps going home with unrejected aid: –
O thoughts that fade into the darkness, straying
alone, afraid!

And hours on end by the grey pond-side kneeling
with little sailing-boat and elbows bare;
forgetting it, because one like it's stealing
below the ripples, but with sails more fair;

and, having still to spare, to share some feeling
with the small sinking face caught sight of there: –
Childhood! Winged likenesses half-guessed at, wheeling,
oh, where, oh, where?

Autumn Day

Lord, it is time. The summer was so great.
Impose upon the sundials now your shadows
and round the meadows let the winds rotate.

Command the last fruits to incarnadine;
vouchsafe, to urge them on into completeness,
yet two more south-like days; and that last sweetness,
inveigle it into the heavy vine.

He'll not build now, who has no house awaiting.
Who's now alone, for long will so remain:
sit late, read, write long letters, and again
return to restlessly perambulating
the avenues of parks when leaves downrain.

Autumn

The leaves are falling, falling as from far,
as though above were withering farthest gardens;
they fall with a denying attitude.

And night by night, down into solitude,
the heavy earth falls far from every star.

We are all falling. This hand's falling too –
all have this falling-sickness none withstands.

And yet there's One whose gently-holding hands
this universal falling can't fall through.

25

Annunciation

(Words of the Angel)

You are not nearer God than we;
he's far from everyone.
And yet your hands most wonderfully
reveal his benison.
From woman's sleeves none ever grew
so ripe, so shimmeringly:
I am the day, I am the dew,
you, Lady, are the Tree.

Pardon, now my long journey's done,
I had forgot to say
what he who sat as in the sun,
grand in his gold array,
told me to tell you, pensive one
(space has bewildered me).
I am the start of what's begun,
you, Lady, are the Tree.

I spread my wings out wide and rose,
the space around grew less;
your little house quite overflows
with my abundant dress.
But still you keep your solitude
and hardly notice me:
I'm but a breeze within the wood,
you, Lady, are the Tree.

The angels tremble in their choir,
grow pale, and separate:
never were longing and desire
so vague and yet so great.
Something perhaps is going to be
that you perceived in dream.
Hail to you! for my soul can see
that you are ripe and teem.

26

You lofty gate, that any day
may open for our good:
you ear my longing songs assay,
my word – I know now – lost its way
in you as in a wood.

And thus your last dream was designed
to be fulfilled by me.
God looked at me: he made me blind . . .

You, Lady, are the Tree.

The Spectator

I watch the storms in the trees above:
after days of mild decaying
my windows shrink from their assaying,
and the things I hear the distance saying,
without a friend I find dismaying,
without a sister cannot love.

There goes the storm to urge and alter,
through forest trees and through time's tree;
and nothing seems to age or falter:
the landscape, like an open psalter,
speaks gravely of eternity.

How small the strife that's occupied us,
how great is all that strives with us!
We might, if, like the things outside us,
we let the great storm over-ride us,
grow spacious and anonymous.

We conquer littleness, obtaining
success that only makes us small,
while, unconstrained and unconstraining,
the permanent eludes us all:

that angel who, though loath, yet lingers
to wrestle with mortality,
and, when opponents' sinews settle
in strife and stretch themselves to metal,
can feel them move beneath his fingers
like strings in some deep melody.

The challenger who failed to stand
that trial so constantly rejected
goes forth upright and resurrected
and great from that hard, forming hand
that clasped about him and completed.
Conquests no longer fascinate.
His growth consists in being defeated
by something ever-grandlier great.

Joshua's Council

As some outflowing river breaks its tether,
pouring in pomp of waters from afar,
so broke upon the elders met together
for the last time the voice of Joshua.

How those who had been laughing were discounted,
how hearts and hands were checked by every man,
as though the din of thirty battles mounted
within one mouth, and that one mouth began.

And once again the thousands were astounded
as on the great day before Jericho,
though now it was in him the trumpets sounded
and their own lives the walls that tottered so

that not till rolling in the pangs of fear,
defencelessly, they seemed to understand
that this was he who, born to domineer,
had shouted to the sun in Gideon: Stand!

And God had gone off in humiliation,
and held the sun, until his hands were tired,
above that immolating generation,
only because one man had so required.

And this was he – whose blood, though they had ceased
to care about him in their calculations,
his five score years and ten had not decreased.
He rose and broke upon their habitations.

Like hail on standing harvests he descended.
What would ye promise God? On every side
uncounted gods await what ye decide.
Choose, and be crushed by Him ye have offended.

And then, with arrogance till then unspoken:
I and my house have been and are his bride.

Whereat they all cried: Help us, give some token,
that this hard choice may not bring punishment.

But they saw him, silent, without pity,
reascending to his mountain city;
then no more. It was the last descent.

The Departure of the Prodigal Son

Now to depart from all this incoherence
that's ours, but which we can't appropriate,
and, like old well-springs, mirrors our appearance
in trembling outlines that disintegrate;
from all this, that with bramble-like adherence
is once more clinging to us – to depart,
and then to start
bestowing on this and that you'd ceased to see
(so took for granted was their ministration)
a sudden gaze: all reconciliation,
tender and close and new-beginningly;
and to divine the whelming desolation,
the inexorable impersonality,
of all that childhood needed to withstand: –
And even then depart, hand out of hand,
as though you tore a wound that had been healing,
and to depart: whither? To unrevealing
distance, to some warm, unrelated land,
that, back-clothwise, will stay, without all feeling,
behind all action: garden, sea or sand;
and to depart: why? Impulse, generation,
impatience, obscure hope, and desperation
not to be understood or understand:

To take on all this, and, in vain persistence.

30

let fall, perhaps, what you have held, to die
alone and destitute, not knowing why –

Is this the way into some new existence?

The Olive Garden

And still he climbed, and through the grey leaves thrust,
quite grey and lost in the grey olive lands,
and laid his burning forehead full of dust
deep in the dustiness of burning hands.

After all, this. And this, then, was the end.
Now I'm to go, while I am going blind,
and, oh, why wilt Thou have me still contend
Thou art, whom I myself no longer find.

No more I find Thee. In myself no tone
of Thee; nor in the rest; nor in this stone.
I can find Thee no more. I am alone.

I am alone with all that human fate
I undertook through Thee to mitigate,
Thou who art not. Oh, shame too consummate . . .

An angel came, those afterwards relate.

Wherefore an angel? Oh, there came the night,
and turned the leaves of trees indifferently,
and the disciples stirred uneasily.
Wherefore an angel? Oh, there came the night.

The night that came requires no specifying;
just so a hundred nights go by,
while dogs are sleeping and while stones are lying –
just any melancholy night that, sighing,
lingers till morning mount the sky.

For angels never come to such men's prayers,
nor nights for them mix glory with their gloom.

Forsakenness is the self-loser's doom,
and such are absent from their father's cares
and disincluded from their mother's womb.

The Poet's Death

He lay. His high-propped face could only peer
in pale rejection at the silent cover,
now that the world and all this knowledge of her,
torn from the senses of her lover,
had fallen back to the unfeeling year.

Those who had seen him living saw no trace
of his deep unity with all that passes;
for these, these valleys here, these meadow-grasses,
these streams of running water, *were* his face.

Oh yes, his face was this remotest distance,
that seeks him still and woos him in despair;
and his mere mask, timidly dying there,
tender and open, has no more consistence
than broken fruit corrupting in the air.

The Cathedral

In those small towns, where clustered round about
old houses squat and jostle like a fair
that's just caught sight of *it*, and then and there
shut up the stalls, and, silenced every shout,

the criers still, the drum-sticks all suspended,
stands gazing up at it with straining ears:
while it, as calm as ever, in the splendid
wrinkled buttress-mantle rears
itself above the homes it never knew:

in those small towns you come to realize
how the cathedrals utterly outgrew
their whole environment. Their birth and rise,
as our own life's too great proximity
will mount beyond our vision and our sense
of other happenings, took precedence
of all things; as though that were history,
piled up in their immeasurable masses
in petrification safe from circumstance,
not that, which down among the dark streets passes
and takes whatever name is given by chance
and goes in that, as children green or red,
or what the dealer has, wear in rotation.
For birth was here, within this deep foundation,
and strength and purpose in this aspiration,
and love, like bread and wine, was all around,
and porches full of lovers' lamentation.
In the tolled hours was heard life's hesitation,
and in those towers that, full of resignation,
ceased all at once from climbing, death was found.

The Panther

Jardin des Plantes, Paris

His gaze, going past those bars, has got so misted
with tiredness, it can take in nothing more.
He feels as though a thousand bars existed,
and no more world beyond them than before.

Those supply powerful paddings, turning there
in tiniest of circles, well might be
the dance of forces round a centre where
some mighty will stands paralyticly.

Just now and then the pupils' noiseless shutter
is lifted. – Then an image will indart,
down through the limbs' intensive stillness flutter,
and end its being in the heart.

33

The Donor

The painters' guild was given this commission.
His Lord, perhaps, he did not really see;
perhaps, as he was kneeling in submission,
no saintly bishop stood in this position
and laid his hand upon him silently.

To kneel like this was everything, maybe
(just as it's all that we ourselves have known):
to kneel: and hold with choking breath one's own
contracted contours, trying to expand,
tight in one's heart like horses in one's hand.

So that, if something awesome should appear,
something unpromised and unprophesied,
we might dare hope it would not see nor hear,
and might approach, until it came quite near,
deep in itself and self-preoccupied.

Roman Sarcophagi

Why should we too, though, not anticipate
(set down here and assigned our places thus)
that only for a short time rage and hate
and this bewildering will remain in us,

as in the ornate sarcophagus, enclosed
with images of gods, rings, glasses, trappings,
there lay in slowly self-consuming wrappings
something being slowly decomposed –

till swallowed by those unknown mouths at last
that never speak. (Where bides a brain that may
yet trust the utterance of its thinking to them?)

Then from the ancient aqueducts there passed
eternal water into them one day: –
that mirrors now and moves and sparkles through them.

A Feminine Destiny

As when, out shooting with his friends, the king
picks up a glass to drink from – any sort –
and afterwards the owner of the thing
preserves it like the rarest ever wrought,

Fate, also thirsty, now and then maybe
has raised a woman to its lips and drunk,
whom then some little life has too much shrunk
from fear of breaking and has carefully

placed in that tremulous vitrine, wherein
its various preciousnesses are consigned
(or objects such as pass for precious there).

As strange as if on loan she's stood therein
and simply gone on growing old and blind
and wasn't precious and was never rare.

Going Blind

She'd sat just like the others there at tea.
And then I'd seemed to notice that her cup
was being a little differently picked up.
She'd smiled once. It had almost hurt to see.

And when eventually they rose and talked
and slowly, and as chance led, were dispersing
through several rooms there, laughing and conversing,
I noticed her. Behind the rest she walked

subduedly, like someone who presently
will have to sing, and with so many listening;
on those bright eyes of hers, with pleasure glistening,
played, as on pools, an outer radiancy.

She followed slowly and she needed time,
as though some long ascent were not yet by;
and yet: as though, when she had ceased to climb,
she would no longer merely walk, but fly.

In a Foreign Park
Borgeby-Gard

Two paths. They're speeding no one's business.
One, though, at times, when pensively alone,
lets you go on. You feel you've lost your bearing;
till suddenly you find you're once more sharing
the solitary round-plot with the stone
and once more reading on it: Baroness
Brite Sophie – and once more with your finger
outfeeling the dilapidated year. –
Why does the newness of this find still linger?

Why do you linger like your first time here
under these elm trees so expectantly,
on this damp, sombre turf none ever treads?

And what's enticing you, contrastingly,
to seek for something in the sunny beds,
as though some rose-tree's name were fascinating?

Why do you stop so? What sound's reaching you?
And why so lostly does your gaze pursue
the butterflies round the tall phlox rotating?

Parting

How I have felt that thing that's called 'to part',
and feel it still: a dark, invincible
cruel something by which what was joined so well
is once more shown, held out, and torn apart.

In what defenceless gaze at that I've stood,
which, as it, calling to me, let me go,
stayed there, as though it were all womanhood,
yet small and white and nothing more than, oh,

a waving, now already unrelated
to me, a slight, continuing wave, – scarce now
explainable: perhaps a plum-tree bough
some perching cuckoo's hastily vacated.

The Courtesan

The sun of Venice in my hair's preparing
a gold where lustrously shall culminate
all alchemy. My brows, which emulate
her bridges, you can contemplate

over the silent perilousness repairing
of eyes which some communion secretly
unites with her canals, so that the sea
rises and ebbs and changes in them. He

who once has seen me falls to envying
my dog, because, in moments of distraction,
this hand no fieriness incinerates,

scathless, bejewelled, there recuperates. –
And many a hopeful youth of high extraction
will not survive my mouth's envenoming.

37

The Steps of the Orangery
Versailles

Like kings who simply pace at certain hours
with no more purpose than the habitude
of showing the double-rank of courtly bowers
their presence in their mantle's solitude – :

even so this flight of steps ascends in lonely
pomp between pillars bowing eternally:
slowly and By the Grace of God and only
to Heaven and nowhere intermediately;

as having ordered all its retinue
to stay behind, – and they're not even daring
to follow at a distance; none may do
so much as hold the heavy train it's wearing.

The Merry-go-Round
Jardin du Luxembourg

With roof and shadow for a while careers
the stud of horses, variously bright,
all from that land that long remains in sight
before it ultimately disappears.
Several indeed pull carriages, with tight-
held rein, but all have boldness in their bearing;
with them a wicked scarlet lion's faring
and now and then an elephant all white.

Just as in woods, a stag comes into view,
save that it has a saddle and tied fast
thereon a little maiden all in blue.

And on the lion a little boy is going,
whose small hot hands hold on with all his might,
while raging lion's tongue and teeth are showing.

And now and then an elephant all white.

And on the horses they come riding past,
girls too, bright-skirted, whom the horse-jumps here
scarce now preoccupy: in full career
elsewhither, hitherwards, a glance they cast –

And now and then an elephant all white.

And this keeps passing by until it's ended,
and hastens aimlessly until it's done.
A red, a green, a grey is apprehended,
a little profile, scarcely yet begun. —
And now and then a smile, for us intended,
blissfully happy, dazzlingly expended
upon this breathless, blindly followed fun . . .

Orpheus. Eurydice. Hermes

That was the strange unfathomed mine of souls.
And they, like silent veins of silver ore,
were winding through its darkness. Between roots
welled up the blood that flows on to mankind,
like blocks of heavy porphyry in the darkness.
Else there was nothing red.

But there were rocks
and ghostly forests. Bridges over voidness
and that immense, grey, unreflecting pool
that hung above its so far distant bed
like a grey rainy sky above a landscape.
And between meadows, soft and full of patience,
appeared the pale strip of the single pathway
like a long line of linen laid to bleach.

And on this single pathway they approached.

In front the slender man in the blue mantle,
gazing in dumb impatience straight before him.

His steps devoured the way in mighty chunks
they did not pause to chew; his hands were hanging,
heavy and clenched, out of the falling folds,
no longer conscious of the lightsome lyre,
the lyre which had grown into his left
like twines of rose into a branch of olive.
It seemed as though his senses were divided:
for, while his sight ran like a dog before him,
turned round, came back, and stood, time and again,
distant and waiting, at the path's next turn,
his hearing lagged behind him like a smell.
It seemed to him at times as though it stretched
back to the progress of those other two
who should be following up this whole ascent.
Then once more there was nothing else behind him
but his climb's echo and his mantle's wind.
He, though, assured himself they still were coming;
said it aloud and heard it die away.
They still were coming, only they were two
that trod with fearful lightness. If he durst
but once look back (if only looking back
were not undoing of this whole enterprise
still to be done), he could not fail to see them,
the two light-footers, following him in silence:

The god of faring and of distant message,
the travelling-hood over his shining eyes,
the slender wand held out before his body,
the wings around his ankles lightly beating,
and in his left hand, as entrusted, *her*.

She, so belov'd, that from a single lyre
more mourning rose than from all women-mourners, –
that a whole world of mourning rose, wherein
all things were once more present: wood and vale
and road and hamlet, field and stream and beast, –
and that around this world of mourning turned,

40

even as around the other earth, a sun
and a whole silent heaven full of stars,
a heaven of mourning with disfigured stars: –
she, so beloved.

But hand in hand now with that god she walked,
her paces circumscribed by lengthy shroudings,
uncertain, gentle, and without impatience.
Wrapt in herself, like one whose time is near,
she thought not of the man who went before them,
nor of the road ascending into life.
Wrapt in herself she wandered. And her deadness
was filling her like fullness.
Full as a fruit with sweetness and with darkness
was she with her great death, which was so new
that for the time she could take nothing in.

She had attained a new virginity
and was intangible; her sex had closed
like a young flower at the approach of evening,
and her pale hands had grown so disaccustomed
to being a wife, that even the slim god's
endlessly gentle contact as he led her
disturbed her like a too great intimacy.

Even now she was no longer that blonde woman
who'd sometimes echoed in the poet's poems,
no longer the broad couch's scent and island,
nor yonder man's possession any longer.

She was already loosened like long hair,
and given far and wide like fallen rain,
and dealt out like a manifold supply.

She was already root.

And when abruptly,
the god had halted her and, with an anguished
outcry, outspoke the words: He has turned round! –
she took in nothing, and said softly: Who?

But in the distance, dark in the bright exit,
someone or other stood, whose countenance
was indistinguishable. Stood and saw
how, on a strip of pathway between meadows,
with sorrow in his look, the god of message
turned silently to go behind the figure
already going back by that same pathway,
its paces circumscribed by lengthy shroudings,
uncertain, gentle, and without impatience.

The Island of the Sirens

Though he told it those whose feast he shared in
(late, by their own scale of time, since they
pried so into perils he had fared in)
more than once, he never found a way

so to startle and with such surprising
words bewitch them, they should come to see
in the blue reposing island-sea,
as he could, those golden isles arising,

sight of which turns peril inside out;
for it's now no longer in the breaking
water's rage, where it was known about.
All without a sound it's overtaking

sailors knowing that on those golden shores there
singing can at times begin, –
and they blindly bend against their oars there,
as hemmed in

by that silence, wherein's all the misted
distance, and by which their ears are fanned
even as though its other side consisted
of the song no mortal can withstand.

The Death of the Beloved

He only knew of death what all men may:
that those it takes it thrusts into dumb night:
When she herself, though, – no, not snatched away,
but tenderly unloosened from his sight,

had glided over to the unknown shades,
and when he felt that he had now resigned
the moonlight of her laughter to their glades,
and all her ways of being kind:

then all at once he came to understand
the dead through her, and joined them in their walk,
kin to them all; he let the others talk,

and paid no heed to them, and called that land
the fortunately-placed, the ever-sweet. –
And groped out all its pathways for her feet.

Adam

He, on the cathedral's steep ascent,
stands and stares near where the window-rose is,
as if awed by the apotheosis
which, when it had reached its full extent,

set him over these and these below.
And he towers and joys in his duration,
plain-resolved; who started cultivation
first of all mankind, and did not know

how he'd find a way from Eden-garden,
ready-filled with all it could supply,
to the new earth. God would only harden,

and, instead of granting him his prayer,
kept on threatening he should surely die.
But the man persisted: She will bear.

Eve

She, on the cathedral's vast ascent,
simply stands there near the window-rose,
with the apple in the apple-pose,
ever henceforth guilty – innocent

of the growingness she brought to birth
since that time she lovingly departed
from the old eternities and started
struggling like a young year through the earth.

Ah, she could have stayed so gladly, though,
just a little longer there, attending
to the sense and concord beasts would show.

But she found the man resolved to go,
so she went out with him, deathwards tending;
and yet God she'd scarcely got to know.

The Site of the Fire

Shunned by the autumn morning, which had got
mistrustful, lay behind the sooty-stemmed
lime trees by which the heath-house had been hemmed
a newness, emptiness. Just one more spot

where children, whence they'd come a mystery,
snatched after rags and filled the air with screams.
But all of them grew quiet whenever he,
the son from here, out of hot, half-charred beams,

with manage of a long forked bough, was trying
to rescue kettles and bent cooking-ware, –
till, looking at them as if he were lying,
he'd bring the others to believe what there,

upon that very spot, once used to stand.
It seemed so strange now it had ceased to be:
fantasticer than Pharoah seemed. And he
was also different. As from some far land.

The Group
Paris

Like someone gathering a quick posy: so
Chance here is hastily arranging faces,
widens and then contracts their interspaces,
seizes two distant, lets a nearer go,

drops this for that, blows weariness away,
rejects, like weed, a dog from the bouquet,
and pulls headforemost what's too low, as through
a maze of stalks and petals, into view,

and binds it in, quite small, upon the hem:
stretches once more to change and separate,
and just has time, for one last look at them,

to spring back to the middle of the mat
on which, in one split second after that,
the glistening lifter's swelling his own weight.

Song of the Sea
Capri, Piccola Marina

Primeval breath from sea,
sea-wind by night;
    you come unseekingly;
one lying till light
must seek and find what he
may interpose:
    primeval breath from sea,

that only blows
as for primeval stone,
pure space
rushing from realms unknown . . .

How felt by a high-sown
fig-tree that clings for place
in the moonlight alone.

The Parks, II

Seized by the lightly alluring
avenues, left and right,
following the reassuring
lead of some beckoning sight,

suddenly you've invaded
the intimacy so deep
a fountain basin, shaded,
and four stone benches keep;

all in a separated
time that goes by alone.
On long-ago vacated
bases of mossy stone

breaths from a tensely gripping
expectancy you mount;
while the silvery dripping
from the sombre fount

talks on, already appearing
sure of your kindredness.
And you feel yourself among hearing
stones, and are motionless.

47

Late Autumn in Venice

The city drifts no longer like a bait now,
upcatching all the days as they emerge.
Brittlier the glassy palaces vibrate now
beneath your gaze. And from each garden verge

the summer like a bunch of puppets dangles,
headforemost, weary, made away.
Out of the ground, though, from dead forest tangles
volition mounts: as though before next day

the sea-commander must have rigged and ready
the galleys in the sleepless Arsenal,
and earliest morning air be tarred already

by an armada, oaringly outpressing,
and suddenly, with flare of flags, possessing
the great wind, radiant and invincible.

Falconry

Emp'ring means unchangedly dominating
many challenges all out of sight:
when the chancellor at dead of night
climbed the tower, he found *him* there, dictating
that bold princely tract on falcon-flight

to the scribe that sat incurvatured;
for in some sequestered gallery
he himself nights long and frequently
had been carrying that still uninured

creature, strange and new and just enseeled.
And then everything had had to yield:
plans which so excitingly upsprung,
chimes deep, deep within him rung

by soft memories he concealed, –
he had spurned them for that timid young

falcon's sake, to enter whose awaring
his attentiveness had never stopped.
Whence he too became a co-ascender
when the bird to which the lordliest render
homage, hoisted from his hand in splendour,
up in that spring morning they were sharing
like an angel on the heron dropped.

Portrait of a Lady of the Eighties

Waiting there against the heavy-weighing
sombre satin drapery,
that above her seems to be displaying
shows of false intensity;

since her scarce-outdistanced girlishnesses
changed with someone else, it might appear:
weary underneath her high-heaped tresses,
inexperienced in her ruche-trimmed dresses,
and as if those folds could overhear

all her homesickness and hesitating
plans for what life now is going to be:
realer, as in novels, scintillating,
full of rapture and fatality, –

to have something safe from all detection
in one's escritoire and, when inclined,
lull oneself in fragrant recollection;
for one's diary at last to find

some beginning that no longer grows,
while one writes, mendacious and unmeaning,
and to wear a petal from a rose
in that heavy, empty locket, leaning

on each indrawn breath. To have at some
time just waved out of the window there –
that would be sufficient and to spare
for this new-ringed hand for months to come.

The Old Lady

White feminine friends in the midst of today
laugh, listen, and plan tomorrow's affairs;
sedater persons sequesteredly weigh
slowly their own particular cares,

the why and the when and the how to do,
and one hears them saying: I think I might; –
she in her lace cap, though, is quite
self-assured, as if she knew

these and the rest were all wrong-headed.
And her fallen chin is bedded
on that white coral through which is threaded
the shawl arranged around her head.

Sometimes, though, at a laugh's outbreaking,
she'll open the springing lids of two waking
looks and exhibit their durable making,
like one from a secret drawer taking
beautiful gems she's inherited.

The Stranger

Careless how it struck those nearest to him,
whose inquiring he'd no longer brook,
once more he departed; lost, forsook. –
For such nights of travel always drew him

stronglier than any lover's night.
How he'd watched in slumberless delight
out beneath the shining stars all yonder
circumscribed horizons roll asunder,
ever-changing like a changing fight;

others, with their moon-bright hamlets tendered
like some booty they had seized, surrendered
peacefully, or through tall trees would shed
glimpses of far-stretching parks, containing
grey ancestral houses that with craning
head a moment he inhabited,
knowing more deeply one could never bide;
then, already round the next curve speeding,
other highways, bridges, landscapes, leading
on to cities darkness magnified.

And to let all this, without all craving,
slip behind him meant beyond compare
more to him than pleasure, goods, or fame.
Though the well-steps in some foreign square,
daily hollowed by the drawers there,
seemed at times like something he could claim.

The Abduction

As a child she'd often eluded the care
of attendants to see the wind and the night
(because inside they are different quite)
at their very beginnings out there;

but no storm-night had so known how
to scatter the giant park before it
as her conscience tore it now,

when down from the silken ladder he caught her
in his arms and further and further brought her . . . :

till the carriage was everything.

And she smelt the black carriage, round which there lay
peril and hot pursuit
ready to spring.
And she found it covered with cold like spray;
and the blackness and coldness were in her too.
Into her hood she crept away
and felt her hair like a friend still true,
and heard estrangedly a stranger say:
I'mherewithyou.

The Bachelor

The family documents illuminated,
and night all round, extending far inside
the shelves. And he was consubstantiated
with his own kin, who now with him outdied.
He felt, the more he read, incorporated
in him their own, in all of them his pride.

The empty chairs upstiffened with hauteur
along the wall, and in the furniture
sheer self-esteems lolled drowsily around.
Down on the French clock gathered night was teeming,
and trembling from its golden mill was streaming
his own time, very finely ground.

He left it there. In order feverishly,
as though he tugged their shrouds from those inditers,
to grab times formerly existent.
Till he was whispering (What, for him, was distant?)
He'd praise some one of those old letter-writers,
as though addressed by him: 'What intuition!'
and beat his arm-chair arms delightedly.
Less inly-limited, the mirror, though,
let now a curtain, now a window go: –
for there stood, almost whole, the apparition.

The Apple Orchard
Borgeby-Gard

Come just after sunset and inspect it,
evening greenness of the new-mown sward:
is it not like something long collected
by ourselves and inwardly upstored,

that we now, from feeling and reviewing,
new hope, jubilation half-forgot,
mixed with inner darkness still, are strewing
out in thoughts before us on this spot,

under trees like Dürer's, that today
bear the weight of work-days uncomputed
in their ripe abundancy enfruited,
serving, patient, finding out the way

that which overtops all measure so
yet may be ingathered and outgiven,
when a long life willingly has striven
to will only that and quietly grow.

The Dog

Up there's the image of a world which glances
are always re-establishing as true.
At times, though, secretly, a thing advances
and stands beside him when he's squeezing through

that image, he so different, down below;
neither excluded nor incorporate,
and squandering, as in doubt, his true estate
upon that image he forgets, although

he still keeps pushing so persistently
his face into it, almost with beseeching,
so close to comprehension, nearly reaching,
and yet renouncing: for he wouldn't *be*.

From Requiem

For Wolf Graf von Kalckreuth

Can I have never seen you? For my heart
feels you like some too-burdensome beginning
one still defers. Oh, could I but begin
to tell of you, dead that you are, you gladly,
you passionately dead. And was it so
alleviating as you supposed, or was
no-more-alive still far from being-dead?
You thought you could possess things better there
where none care for possessions. You supposed
that over there you'd be inside the landscape
that here closed up before you like a picture,
would enter the beloved from within
and penetrate through all things, strong and wheeling.
Oh, that you may not have too long had cause
to tax your boyish error with deception!
Loosened within that rush of melancholy,
ecstatically and only half-aware,
may you, in motion round the distant stars,
have found the happiness that you transposed
from here into that being-dead you dreamt of.
How near you were to it, dear friend, even here.
How much it was at home here, what you purposed,
the earnest joy of your so strenuous longing.
When, tired of being happy and unhappy,
you mined into yourself and painfully
climbed with an insight, almost breaking down
under the weight of dark discovery:
you carried what you never recognized,
you carried joy, you carried through your blood
your little saviour's burden to the shore.

Why did you not wait till the difficult

gets quite unbearable: until it turns,
and is so difficult because so real?
That was perhaps your next allotted moment;
it may perhaps have been already trimming
its garland at the door you slammed for ever.

    Oh that percussion, how it penetrates,
when somewhere, through impatience's sharp draught,
something wide open shuts and locks itself!
Who can deny on oath that in the earth
a crack goes springing through the healthy seeds?
Who has investigated if tame beasts
are not convulsed with sudden lust for killing
when that jerk shoots like lightning through their brains?
Who can deduce the influence leaping out
from actions to some near-by terminal?
Who can conduct where everything's conductive?

    The fact that you destroyed. That this must be
related of you till the end of time.
Even if a hero's coming, who shall tear
meaning we take to be the face of things
off like a mask and in a restless rage
reveal us faces whose mute eyes have long
been gazing at us through dissembling holes:
this is sheer face and will not be transfigured:
that you destroyed. For blocks were lying there,
and in the air already was the rhythm
of some now scarce repressible construction.
You walked around and did not see their order,
one hid the other from you; each of them
seemed to be rooted, when in passing by
you tried at it, with no real confidence
that you could lift it. And in desperation
you lifted every one of them, but only
to sling them back into the gaping quarry
wherein, being so distended by your heart,
they would no longer fit. Had but a woman
laid her light hand on the still mild beginning

of this dark rage; had someone occupied,
occupied in the inmost of his being,
but quietly met you on your dumb departure
to do this deed; had even something led you
to take your journey past some wakeful workshop
where men were hammering and day achieving
simple reality; had there been room
enough in your full gaze to let the image
even of a toiling beetle find admittance:
then, in a sudden flash of intuition,
you would have read that script whose characters
you'd slowly graved into yourself since childhood,
trying from time to time whether a sentence
might not be formed: alas, it seemed unmeaning.
I know; I know: you lay in front and thumbed
away the grooves, like someone feeling out
the inscription on a grave-stone. Anything
that seemed to give a light you held as lamp
before those letters; but the flame went out
before you'd understood – your breath, perhaps,
perhaps the trembling of your hand; perhaps
just of its own accord, as flames will do.
You never read it. And we do not dare
to read through all the sorrow and the distance.

We only watch the poems that still climb,
still cross, the inclination of your feeling,
carrying the words that you had chosen. No,
you did not choose all; often a beginning
was given you in full, and you'd repeat it
like some commission. And you thought it sad.
Ah, would you had never heard it from yourself!
Your angel sounds on, uttering the same
text with a different accent, and rejoicing
breaks out in me to hear his recitation,
rejoicing over you: for this was yours:
that from you every proffered love fell back,

that you had recognized renunciation
as price of seeing and in death your progress.
This was what you possessed, you artist, these
three open moulds. Look, here is the casting
from the first: space for your feeling; and look, there,
from the second I'll strike out for you the gaze
that craves for nothing, the great artist's gaze;
and in the third, which you yourself broke up
too soon, and which as yet the first outrushing
of quivering feed from the white-heated heart
had scarce had time to reach, a death was moulded,
deepened by genuine labour, that own death
which has such need of us because we live it,
and which we're nowhere nearer to than here.

All this was your possession and your friendship;
as you yourself often divined; but then
the hollowness of those moulds frightened you,
you groped within and drew up emptiness
and mourned your lot. – O ancient curse of poets!
Being sorry for themselves instead of saying,
for ever passing judgment on their feeling
instead of shaping it; for ever thinking
that what is sad or joyful in themselves
is what they know and what in poems may fitly
be mourned or celebrated. Invalids,
using a language full of woefulness
to tell us where it hurts, instead of sternly
transmuting into words those selves of theirs,
as imperturbable cathedral carvers
transposed themselves into the constant stone.

That would have been salvation. Had you once
perceived how fate may pass into a verse
and not come back, how, once in, it turns image,
nothing but image, but an ancestor,
who sometimes, when you watch him in his frame,
seems to be like you and again not like you: –
you would have persevered.

But this is petty,
thinking of what was not. And some appearance
of undeserved reproach in these comparings.
Whatever happens has had such a start
of our supposing that we never catch it,
never experience what it really looked like.
    Don't be ashamed, when the dead brush against you,
those other dead, who held out to the end.
(What, after all, does end mean?) Exchange glances
peacefully with them, as is customary,
and have no fear of being conspicuous
through carrying the burden of our grief.
The big words from those ages when as yet
happening was visible are not for us.
Who talks of victory? To endure is all.

From The Duino Elegies

First Elegy

Who, if I cried, would hear me among the angelic
orders? And even if one of them suddenly
pressed me against his heart, I should fade in the strength
    of his
stronger existence. For Beauty's nothing
but beginning of Terror we're still just able to bear,
and why we adore it so is because it serenely
disdains to destroy us. Every angel is terrible.
And so I repress myself, and swallow the call-note
of depth-dark sobbing. Alas, who is there
we can make use of? Not angels, not men;
and even the noticing beasts are aware
that we don't feel very securely at home
in this interpreted world. There remains, perhaps,
some tree on a slope, to be looked at day after day,
there remains for us yesterday's walk and the long-drawn
    loyalty
of a habit that liked us and stayed and never gave notice.
Oh, and there's Night, there's Night, when wind full of
    cosmic space
feeds on our faces: for whom would she not remain,
longed for, mild disenchantress, painfully there
for the lonely heart to achieve? Is she lighter for lovers?
Alas, with each other they only conceal their lot!
Don't you know *yet*? – Fling the emptiness out of your
    arms
to broaden the spaces we breathe – maybe that the birds
will feel the extended air in more fervent flight.

Yes, the Springs had need of you. Many a star
was waiting for you to perceive it. Many a wave
would rise in the past towards you; or else, perhaps,

as you went by an open window, a violin
would be utterly giving itself. All this was commission.
But were you equal to it? Were you not still
distraught by expectancy, as though all were announcing
some beloved's approach? (As if you could hope
to house her, with all those great strange thoughts
going in and out and often staying overnight!)
Should you be longing, though, sing the great lovers: the
    fame
of all they can feel is far from immortal enough.
Those – you envied them almost, those forsaken, you
    found
so far beyond the requited in loving. Begin
ever anew their never-attainable praise.
Consider: the Hero continues, even his setting
was a pretext for further existence, an ultimate birth.
But lovers are taken back by exhausted Nature
into herself, as though such creative force
could not be exerted twice. Does Gaspara Stampa
mean enough to you yet, and that any girl, whose beloved
has slipped away, might feel, from that far intenser
example of loving: 'Could I but become like her!'?
Should not these oldest sufferings be finally growing
fruitfuller for us? Is it not time that, in loving,
we freed ourselves from the loved one, and, quivering,
    endured:
as the arrow endures the string, to become, in the gathering
    out-leap,
something more than itself? For staying is nowhere.

Voices, voices. Hearken, my heart, as only
saints once hearkened: so, that the giant call
lifted them off the ground; they, though, impossibles,
went on kneeling and paid no heed:
such was their hearkening. Not that you could bear God's
voice, by a long way. But hark to the suspiration,
the uninterrupted news that grows out of silence.

Rustling towards you now from those youthfully-dead.
Whenever you entered a church in Rome or in Naples
were you not always being quietly addressed by their fate?
Or else an inscription sublimely imposed itself on you,
as, lately, the tablet in Santa Maria Formosa.
What they require of me? that I should gently remove
the appearance of suffered injustice, that hinders
a little, at times, their purely-proceeding spirits.

True, it is strange to inhabit the earth no longer,
to use no longer customs scarcely acquired,
not to interpret roses, and other things
that promise so much, in terms of a human future;
to be no longer all that one used to be
in endlessly anxious hands, and to lay aside
even one's proper name like a broken toy.
Strange, not to go on wishing one's wishes. Strange,
to see all that was once relation so loosely fluttering
hither and thither in space. And it's hard, being dead,
and full of retrieving before one begins to perceive
a little eternity. – All of the living, though,
make the mistake of drawing too sharp distinctions.
Angels (it's said) would be often unable to tell
whether they moved among living or dead. The eternal
torrent whirls all the ages through either realm
for ever, and sounds above their voices in both.

They've finally no more need of us, the early-departed,
one's gently weaned from terrestrial things as one mildly
outgrows the breasts of a mother. But we, that have need of
such mighty secrets, we, for whom sorrow's so often
source of blessedest progress, could we exist without
    them?
Is the story in vain, how once, in the mourning for Linos,
venturing earliest music pierced barren numbness, and how,
in the startled space an almost deified youth
suddenly quitted for ever, emptiness first
felt the vibration that now lifts us and comforts and helps?

The Ninth Elegy

Why, when this span of life might be fleeted away
as laurel, a little darker than all
the surrounding green, with tiny waves on the border
of every leaf (like the smile of a wind): – oh, why
have to be human, and, shunning Destiny,
long for Destiny? . . .
                              Not because happiness really
exists, that precipitate profit of imminent loss.
Not out of curiosity, not just to practise the heart,
that could still be there in laurel. . . .
But because being here is much, and because all this
that's here, so fleeting, seems to require us and strangely
concerns us. Us the most fleeting of all. Just once,
everything, only for once. Once and no more. And we, too,
once. And never again. But this
having been once, though only once,
having been once on earth – can it ever be cancelled?

And so we keep pressing on and trying to perform it,
trying to contain it within our simple hands,
in the more and more crowded gaze, in the speechless
      heart.
Trying to become it. To give it to whom? We'd rather
hold on to it all for ever . . . But into the other relation,
what, alas! do we carry across? Not the beholding we've
      here
slowly acquired, and no here occurrence. Not one.
Sufferings, then. Above all, the hardness of life,
the long experience of love; in fact,
purely untellable things. But later,
under the stars, what use? the more deeply untellable
      stars?
Yet the wanderer too doesn't bring from mountain to
      valley

63

a handful of earth; of for all untellable earth, but only
a word he has won, pure, the yellow and blue
gentian. Are we, perhaps, *here* just for saying: House,
Bridge, Fountain, Gate, Jug, Fruit tree, Window, –
possibly: Pillar, Tower? . . . but for *saying*, remember,
oh, for such saying as never the things themselves
hoped so intensely to be. Is not the secret purpose
of this sly Earth, in urging a pair of lovers,
just to make everything leap with ecstasy in them?
Threshold: what does it mean
to a pair of lovers, that they should be wearing their own
worn threshold a little, they too, after the many before,
before the many to come, . . . as a matter of course!

Here is the time for the Tellable, *here* is its home.
Speak and proclaim. More than ever
things we can live with are falling away, for that
which is oustingly taking their place is an imageless act.
Act under crusts, that will readily split as soon
as the doing within outgrows them and takes a new outline.
Between the hammers lives on
our heart, as between the teeth
the tongue, which, in spite of all,
still continues to praise.

Praise this world to the Angel, not the untellable: you
can't impress him with the splendour you've felt; in the
 cosmos
where he more feelingly feels you're only a novice. So
 show him
some simple thing, refashioned by age after age,
till it lives in our hands and eyes as a part of ourselves.
Tell him *things*. He'll stand more astonished: as you did
beside the roper in Rome or the potter in Egypt.
Show him how happy a thing can be, how guileless and
 ours;
how even the moaning of grief purely determines on form,
serves as a thing, or dies into a thing, – to escape

to a bliss beyond the fiddle. These things that live on
    departure
understand when you praise them: fleeting, they look for
rescue through something in us, the most fleeting of all.
Want us to change them entirely, within our invisible
    hearts,
into – oh, endlessly – into ourselves! Whosoever we are.

Earth, is it not just this that you want: to arise
invisibly in us? Is not your dream
to be one day invisible? Earth! invisible!
What is your urgent command, if not transformation?
Earth, you darling, I will! Oh, believe me, you need
no more of your spring-times to win me over: a single one,
ah, one, is already more than my blood can endure.
Beyond all names I am yours, and have been for ages.
You were always right, and your holiest inspiration
is Death, that friendly Death.
Look, I am living. On what? Neither childhood nor future
are growing less. . . . Supernumerous existence
wells up in my heart.

VII

Praising, that's it! As a praiser and blesser
he came like the ore from the taciturn mine.
Came with his heart, oh, transient presser,
for men, of a never-exhaustible wine.

Voice never fails him for things lacking lustre,
sacred example will open his mouth.
All becomes vineyard, all becomes cluster,
warmed by his sympathy's ripening south.

Crypts and the mouldering kings who lie there
do not belie his praising, neither
doubt, when a shadow obscures our days.

He is a messenger always attendant,
reaching far through their gates resplendent
dishes of fruit for the dead to praise.

IX

Only by him with whose lays
shades were enraptured
may the celestial praise
faintly be captured.

Only who tasted their own
flower with the sleeping
holds the most fugitive tone
ever in keeping.

Make but that image the pond

IX

fleetingly tendered
knownly endure!

Not till both here and beyond
voices are rendered
lasting and pure.

XXIII

Only when flight shall soar
not for its own sake only
up into heaven's lonely
silence, and be no more

merely the lightly profiling,
proudly successful tool,
playmate of winds, beguiling
time there, careless and cool:

only when some pure Whither
outweighs boyish insistence
on the achieved machine

will who has journeyed thither
be, in that fading distance,
all that his flight has been.

XXVI

You that could sound till the end, though, immortal
accorder,
seized by the scorn-maddened Maenads' intemperate
throng,
wholly outsounded their cries when in musical order
soared from the swarm of deformers your formative song.

FROM THE SONNETS TO ORPHEUS: FIRST PART

Wrestle and rage as they might on that fated career,
none was able to shatter your head or your lyre:
hard stones hurled at your heart could only acquire
gentleness, soon as they struck you, and power to hear.

Though they destroyed you at last and revenge had its will,
sound of you lingered in lions and rocks you were first to
enthral, in the trees and the birds. You are singing there
    still.

O you god that has vanished! You infinite track!
Only because dismembering hatred dispersed you
are we hearers today and a mouth which else Nature would
    lack.

IV

This is the creature there has never been.
They never knew it, and yet, none the less,
they loved the way it moved, its suppleness,
its neck, its very gaze, mild and serene.

Not there, because they loved it, it behaved
as though it were. They always left some space.
And in that clear unpeopled space they saved
it lightly reared its head, with scarce a trace

of not being there. They fed it, not with corn,
but only with the possibility
of being. And that was able to confer

such strength, its brow put forth a horn. One horn.
Whitely it stole up to a maid, – to *be*
within the silver mirror and in her.

X

Long will machinery menace the whole of our treasure,
while it, unmindful of us, dares to a mind of its own.
Checking the glorious hand's flaunting of lovelier leisure,
now for some stubborner work sternlier it fashions the stone.

Not for an hour will it stay, so that for once we may flee it,
oiling itself in a quiet factory, fitly employed.
Now it is life, no less, and feels best able to be it,

having, with equal resolve, ordered, constructed, destroyed.

Even today, though, existence is magical, pouring
freshly from hundreds of well-springs, – a playing of purest
forces, which none can surprise without humbly adoring.

Words still melt into something beyond their embrace . . .
Music, too, keeps building anew with the insecurest
stones her celestial house in unusable space.

XV

O fountain mouth, you mouth that can respond
so inexhaustibly to all who ask
with one, pure, single saying. Marble mask
before the water's flowing face. Beyond,

the aqueducts' long derivation. Past
the tombs, from where the Apennines begin,
they bring your saying to you, which at last,
over the grizzled age of your dark chin,

falls to the waiting basin, crystal-clear;
falls to the slumbering recumbent ear,
the marble ear, with which you still confer.

One of earth's ears. With her own lonely mood
she thus converses. Let a jug intrude,
she'll only think you've interrupted her.

XVII

Where, in what ever-blissfully watered gardens, upon what
    trees,
out of, oh, what gently dispetalled flower-cups do these
so strange-looking fruits of consolation mature?
Delicious, when, now and then, you pick one up in the poor

trampled field of your poverty. Time and again you find
yourself lost in wonder over the size of the fruit,
over its wholesomeness, over its smooth, soft rind,
and that neither the heedless bird above nor jealous worm at
    the root

has been before you. Are there, then, trees where angels will
    congregate,
trees invisible leisurely gardeners so curiously cultivate,
that, without being ours, they bear for us fruits like those?

Have we, then, never been able, we shadows and shades,
with our doing that ripens too early and then as suddenly
    fades,
to disturb that even-tempered summer's repose?

The Raising of Lazarus

One had to bear with the majority –
what they wanted was a sign that screamed:
Martha, though, and Mary – he had dreamed
they would be contented just to see
that he *could*. But not a soul believed him:
'Lord, you've come too late,' said all the crowd.
So to peaceful Nature, though it grieved him,
on he went to do the unallowed.
Asked them, eyes half-shut, his body glowing
with anger, 'Where's the grave?' Tormentedly.
And to them it seemed his tears were flowing,
as they thronged behind him, curiously.
As he walked, the thing seemed monstrous to him,
childish, horrible experiment:
then there suddenly went flaming through him
such an all-consuming argument
against their life, their death, their whole collection
of separations made by them alone,
all his body quivered with rejection
as he gave out hoarsely 'Raise the stone'.
Someone shouted that the corpse was stinking
(buried now four days ago) – but He
stood erect, brim-full of that unblinking,
mounting gesture, that so painfully
lifted up his hand (no hand was ever
raised so slowly, so immeasurably),
till it stood there, shining in the gloom.
There it slowly, clawingly contracted:
what if all the dead should be attracted
upwards, through that syphon of a tomb,
where a pallid chrysalidal thing

was writhing up from where it had been lying? –
But it stood alone (no more replying),
and they saw vague, unidentifying
Life compelled to give it harbouring.

The Spirit Ariel

(After reading Shakespeare's *Tempest*)

Sometime, somewhere, it had set him free,
that jerk with which you flung yourself in youth
full upon greatness, far from all respect.
Then he grew willing: and since then a servant,
after each service waiting for his freedom.
Half-domineering, half almost ashamed,
you make excuses, that for this and this
you still require him, and insist, alas!
how you have helped him. Though you feel
        yourself
how everything detained by his detention
is missing from the air. Sweet and seductive,
to let him go, and then, abjuring magic,
entering into destiny like others,
to know that henceforth his most gentle friendship,
without all tension, nowhere bound by duty,
a something added to the space we breathe,
is busied heedless in the element.
Dependent now, having more the gift
to form the dull mouth to that conjuration
that brought him headlong. Powerless, ageing, poor,
yet breathing *him*, incomprehensibly
far-scattered fragrance, making the Invisible
at last complete. Smiling, to think you'd been
on nodding terms with that, such great acquaintance
so soon familiar. Perhaps weeping, too,
when you remember how it loved you and
would yet be going, always both at once.

(And there I left it? Now he terrifies me,
this man who's duke again. – The ways he draws
the wire into his head, and hangs himself
beside the other puppets, and henceforth
begs mercy of the play! . . . What epilogue
of achieved mastery! Putting off, standing there
with only one's own strength: 'which is most faint'.)

Shatter Me, Music

Shatter me, music, with rhythmical fury!
Lofty reproach, lifted against the heart
that feared such surge of perception, sparing itself. My heart,
    – there:
behold your glory! Can you remain contented
with less expansive beats, when the uppermost arches
are waiting for you to fill them with organing impulse?
Why do you long for the face withheld, for the far beloved?
For, oh, if your longing lacks breath to extort resounding
    storms
from the trumpet an angel blows on high at the end of the
    world,
she also does not exist, nowhere, will never be born,
she whom you parchingly miss . . .

Behind the Innocent Trees

Behind the innocent trees
old Fate is slowly forming
her taciturn face.
Wrinkles travel thither . . .
Here a bird screams, and there

74

a furrow of pain
shoots from the hard sooth-saying mouth.

Oh, and the almost lovers,
with their unvaledictory smiles! –
their destiny setting and rising above them,
constellational,
night-enraptured.
Not yet proffering itself to their experience,
it still remains,
hovering in heaven's paths,
an airy form.

The Great Night

I'd often stand at the window started the day before,
stand and stare at you. It still seemed to warn me off,
the strange city, whose unconfiding landscape
gloomed as though I didn't exist. The nearest
things didn't mind if I misunderstood them. The street
would thrust itself up to the lamp, and I'd see it was strange.
A sympathisable room up there, revealed in the lamplight:
I'd begin to share: they'd notice, and close the shutters.
I'd stand. Then a child would cry, and I'd know the mothers
in the houses, what they availed, and I'd know as well
the inconsolable grounds of infinite crying.
Or else a voice would sing, and what was expected
be just a little surpassed; or an old man coughed below,
full of reproach, as his body were in the right
against a gentler world. Or else, when an hour was striking,
I'd begin to count too late and let it escape me.
As a strange little boy, when at last they invite him to join
        them,
cannot catch the ball, and is quite unable
to share the game the rest are so easily playing,
but stands and gazes – whither? – I'd stand, and, all at once,

75

realize *you* were being friends with me, playing with me,
    grown-up
Night, and I'd gaze at you. While towers
were raging, and while, with its hidden fate,
a city stood round me, and undivinable mountains
camped against me, and Strangeness, in narrowing circles,
hungrily prowled round my casual flares of perception:
then, lofty Night,
you were not ashamed to recognize me. Your breathing
went over me; your smile upon all that spacious
consequence passed into me.

Beloved, Lost to Begin With

Beloved,
lost to begin with, never greeted,
I do not know what tones most please you.
No more when the future's wave hangs poised is it you
I try to discern there. All the greatest
images in me, far-off experienced landscape,
towers and towns and bridges and un-
suspected turns of the way,
and the power of those lands once intertwined
with the life of the gods:
mount up within me to mean
you, who forever elude.

Oh, you are the gardens!
Oh, with such yearning
hope I watched them! An open window
in a country house, and you almost stepped out
thoughtfully to meet me. Streets I discovered, –
you had just walked down them,
and sometimes in dealers' shops the mirrors,
still dizzy with you, returned with a start
my too-sudden image. – Who knows whether the

self-same bird didn't ring through each of us,
separately, yesterday evening?

Exposed on the Heart's Mountains

Exposed on the heart's mountains. Look, how small there!
look, the last hamlet of words, and, higher,
(but still how small!) yet one remaining ·
farmstead of feeling: d'you see it?
Exposed on the heart's mountains. Virgin rock
under the hands. Though even here
something blooms: from the dumb precipice
an unknowing plant blooms singing into the air.
But what of the knower? Ah, he began to know
and holds his peace, exposed on the heart's mountains.
While, with undivided mind,
many, maybe, many well-assured mountain beasts,
pass there and pause. And the mighty sheltered bird
circles the summits' pure refusal. – But, oh,
no longer sheltered, here on the heart's mountains ...

Time and Again

Time and again, however well we know the landscape of
        love,
and the little church-yard with lamenting names,
and the frightfully silent ravine wherein all the others
end: time and again we go out two together,
under the old trees, lie down again and again
between the flowers, face to face with the sky.

To Music

(The property of Frau Hanna Wolff)

Music: breathing of statues. Perhaps:
stillness of pictures. You speech, where speeches
end. You time,
vertically poised on the courses of vanishing hearts.

Feelings for what? Oh, you transformation
of feelings into ... audible landscape!
You stranger: Music. Space that's outgrown us,
heart-space. Innermost ours,
that, passing our limits, outsurges, –
holiest parting:
where what is within surrounds us
as practised horizon, as other
side of the air,
pure,
gigantic,
no longer lived in.

From the Poems of Count C.W.

Karnak. We'd ridden, dinner quickly done with,
Hélène and I, to get the moonlight view.
The dragoman pulled up: the Avenue, –
the Pylon, ah! I'd never felt so one with

the lunar world! (Are you being magnified
within me, greatness, then beyond control?)
Is travel – seeking? Well, this was a goal.
The watchman at the entrance first supplied

the frightening scale. How lowly seemed his station
beside the gate's unchecked self-exaltation!
And then, for a whole life-time's meditation
did not the Column bring enough and more?

Ruin vindicated it: it would have been
too high for highest roof. It stood and bore
Egyptian night.
                    The following fellaheen

now fell behind us. To get over this
took time, because it almost stopped the heart
to know that such out-standing formed a part
of that same being we died in. – If I had
a son, I'd send him, when our only care
is finding truth to live by: 'Charles, it's there, –
walk through the Pylon, stand and look, my lad.'

Why could it not help *us* more helpfully?
That we endured it was enough indeed:
you in your travelling dress, the invalid,
and I the hermit in my theory.

And yet, the mercy! Can you still recall
that lake round which the granite cats were seated?
Mark-stones (of what?). So chained, as by repeated
spells, into that enchanted rectangle

one felt, that had not five been overturned
along one side (you too were overcome),
they would that moment, cattish, stony, dumb,
have held a court of judgment.

                              All discerned
was judgment. Here the ban upon the pond,
there on the margin the giant scarabee,
along the walls the epic history
of monarchs: judgment. And yet, quite beyond

all comprehension, an acquittal too.
As figure after figure there was filled
with the pure moonlight, the relief, outdrilled
in clearest outline, hollow, trough-like, grew

so much receptacle – for nothing less
than what, though never hidden, none could see,
for the world-secret, so essentially
secret, it baffles all secretiveness!

All books keep turning past it: no one ever
read in a book a thing so manifest
(I want a word – how can it be expressed?):
the Immeasurable submitted to the measure

of sacrifice. – Look there, oh, look: what's keeping,
that has not learnt to give itself away?
All things are passing. Help them on their way.
And then your life will not be merely seeping

out through some crack. Remain your whole life long
the conscious giver. Mule and cow, they throng
in close procession to the spot where he,
the god-king, like a stilled child, peaceably

receives and smiles. His mighty sacredness
is never out of breath. He takes and takes:
and yet such mitigation overtakes,
that the papyrus flower by the princess

is often merely clasped, not broken. –
                                        Here
all ways of sacrifice abruptly end,
the Sabbath starts, the long weeks comprehend
its mind no longer. Man and beast appear

to keep at times some gains from the god's eyes.
Profit, though difficult, can be secured;
one tries and tries, the earth can be procured,
who, though, but gives the price gives up the prize.

Meaningful Word, 'Inclination'

Meaningful word, 'inclination'! Would we were aware of
it everywhere, not just in hearts where we think it's con-
    cealed!
That of a hill, when it slowly, with gathering share of
growth, inclines to the welcoming field:
let what we are by increasing of that be exceeded;
let but the small bird's liberal flight
gift us with heart-space, making a future unneeded!
All is abundance. Oh, there was quite
enough even then when Childhood almost defeated
with endless existence. Life had poured
more than sufficient. How could we ever be cheated,
ever betrayed, we with every reward
over-rewarded? . . .

Strongest Star

Strongest star, not needing to await
specious aid from Darkness, whom the rest
need to make their darkness manifest
Star already setting, consummate,

when the others but begin their wheeling
through the gradually expanding night.
Star of love's priestesses, star whom feeling
kindles of itself into a light

ever-candid, never carbonising:
you that, sinking down the solar line,
overtake such infinite arising
with the purity of your decline.

The Fruit

It climbed and climbed from earth invisibly,
and kept its secret in the silent stem,
and turned in the clear blossom into flame,
and then resumed its secrecy.

And through a whole long summer fructified
within that day and night travailing tree,
and felt itself as urging instancy
to meet responding space outside.

And though it now displays so shiningly
that rondure of completed rest anew,
within the rind it sinks resigningly
back to the centre it outgrew.

Early Spring

Harshness gone. And sudden mitigation
laid upon the field's uncovered grey.
Little runnels change their intonation.
Tentative caresses stray

round the still earth from immensity.
Roads run far into the land, foretelling.
Unexpectedly you find it, welling
upwards in the empty tree.

Gods, For All We Can Tell

Gods, for all we can tell,   stride as richly bestowing now as
    in former years;
gently their wind as well   reaches our harvests, blowing over
    more loaded ears.

Quite to forget it will fail   quite to elude the relation: they
  will perform their share.
Suddenly, silently there,   prizing your proudest creation,
  ponders their different scale.

The Sap is Mounting Back

The sap is mounting back from that unseenness
darkly renewing in the common deep,
back to the light, and feeding the pure greenness
hiding in rinds round which the winds still weep.

The inner side of Nature is reviving,
another *sursum corda* will resound;
invisibly, a whole year's youth is striving
to climb those trees that look so iron-bound

Preserving still that grey and cool expression,
the ancient walnut's filling with event;
while the young brush-wood trembles with repression
under the perching bird's presentiment.

On the Sunny Road

On the sunny road, within the hollow
cloven tree, that now for generations
has been a trough, inaudibly renewing
a little film of water, I can still my
thirst by letting all that pristine freshness
ripple from my wrists through all my body.
Drinking were too much for me, too open:
this, though, this procrastinating gesture
fills my consciousness with sparkling water.

So, if you came, I could be contented
just to let my hands rest very lightly
either on your shoulder's youthful rounding
or upon your breasts' responsive pressure.

The One Birds Plunge Through

The one birds plunge through's not that trusty space
where each confided form's intensified.
(Out in the open there you're self-denied,
and go on vanishing without a trace.)

Space spreads transposingly from us to things:
really to feel the way a tree upsprings,
cast round it space from that which inwardly
expands in you. Surround it with retention.
It has no bounds. Not till its reascension
in your renouncing is it truly tree.

For Count Karl Lanckoronski

'*No intellect, no ardour is redundant*':
to make one through the other more abundant
is what we're for, and some are singled out
for purest victory in that contention:
no signal can escape their tried attention,
their hands are wieldy and their weapons stout.

No sound must be too soft for their detection,
they must perceive that angle of deflection
to which the dial-pointer scarcely stirs,
and must, as might be with their eyelids, utter
reply to what the butterflies out-flutter
and learn to fathom what a flower infers.

84

No less than others they can be extinguished,
and yet they must (why else were they distinguished?)
feel even with catastrophe some kin,
and, while the rest are helplessly bewailing,
recapture in the strokes of each assailing
the rhythm of some stoniness within.

They must be stationed like a shepherd, keeping
his lonely watch: one might suppose him weeping,
till, coming close, one feels his piercing sight;
and, as for him the speech of stars is clear,
for them must be as intimately near
what climbs in still procession through the night.

In slumber also they continue seers:
from dream and being, from laughter and from tears
a meaning gathers ... which if they can seize,
and kneel to Life and Death in adoration,
another measure for the whole creation
is given us in those right-angled knees.

Epitaph

R. M. R.

4 DECEMBER 1875 – 29 DECEMBER 1926

ROSE, OH THE PURE CONTRADICTION, DELIGHT
OF BEING NO ONE'S SLEEP UNDER SO MANY LIDS.

Notes on the Poems

The day is coming when from God the Tree. Der Ast vom Baume Gott, der über Italien reicht

The 34th poem of the First Book ('The Book of the Monastic Life') of *The Book of Hours* (1905). The poem's setting is Russia, and this section of the *Stundenbuch* was composed in the autumn of 1899.

From THE BOOK OF IMAGES (1902 and 1906).
Das Buch der Bilder

Childhood. Kindheit
  Written in the winter of 1905–6.

Autumn Day. Herbsttag
  Paris, 21 September 1902.

Autumn. Herbst
  Paris, 11 September 1902

Annunciation. Verkündigung (Die Worte des Engels)
  21 July 1899.

The Spectator. Der Schauende
  January 1901.

From NEW POEMS: FIRST PART (1907).
Neue Gedichte

Joshua's Council. Josuas Landtag
  July 1906.

The Departure of the Prodigal Son. Der Auszug des verlorenen Sohnes
  June 1906.

The Olive Garden. Der Ölbaumgarten
May–June 1906.

The Poet's Death. Der Tod des Dichters
May–June 1906.

The Cathedral. Die Kathedrale
1 July 1906.

The Panther. Der Panther (Im Jardin des Plantes, Paris)
1903, or possibly late 1902.

The Donor. Der Stifter
July 1906.

Roman Sarcophagi. Römische Sarkophage
In many Italian towns and villages stone sarcophagi are used
as troughs or basins, from which running water may be drawn.
Written in Paris, May–June 1906.

A Feminine Destiny. Ein Frauenschicksal
1 July 1906.

Going Blind. Die Erblindende
June 1906.

In a Foreign Park. In einem fremden Park
Mid-July 1906.

Parting. Abschied
Early 1906.

The Courtesan. Die Courtisane
Capri, mid-March 1907.

The Steps of the Orangery. Die Treppe der Orangerie
Paris, mid-July 1906.

The Merry-go-Round. Das Karussell
The image in lines 3/4 is that of a coastline gradually slipping
below the horizon, as seen by the voyager. Written in Paris,
June 1906.

Orpheus. Eurydice. Hermes. Orpheus. Eurydike. Hermes
Written 1904.

NOTES ON THE POEMS

From NEW POEMS: SECOND PART (1908).
Der neuen Gedichte anderer Teil

The Island of the Sirens. Die Insel der Sirenen
Paris, between 22 August and 5 September 1907.

The Death of the Beloved. Der Tod der Geliebten
August–September 1907.

Adam. Adam
Paris, summer 1908.

Eve. Eva
Summer 1908.

The Site of the Fire. Die Brandstätte
Summer 1908.

The Group. Die Gruppe (Paris)
Summer 1908.

Song of the Sea. Lied vom Meer
Capri, January 1907.

The Parks, II. Die Parke II
August 1907.

Late Autumn in Venice. Spätherbst in Venedig
Paris, summer 1908.

Falconry. Falkenbeize
   The Emperor Frederick II ('*stupor mundi*'), 1194–1250, composed a treatise on falconry which is still recognized as the most authoritative ever written. The third stanza refers to a process known as 'to enseel' (Old French *ciller*, from *cil*, eyelash). By this the eyelids of a newly-captured falcon or hawk were stitched up with a needle and thread, until the bird had become accustomed to its captor and to captivity. Written in Paris, summer 1908.

Portrait of a Lady of the Eighties. Damenbildnis aus den achtziger Jahren
   August–September 1907.

The Old Lady. Die Greisin
Summer 1908.

The Stranger. Der Fremde
Summer 1908.

The Abduction. Die Entführung
Summer 1908.

The Bachelor. Der Junggeselle
Summer 1908.

The Apple-Orchard. Der Apfelgarten
2 August 1907.

The Dog. Der Hund
June–July 1907.

From REQUIEM (1909).

For Wolf Graf von Kalckreuth. Für Wolf Graf von Kalckreuth
Wolf Graf von Kalckreuth (1887–1906) was a translator of
Baudelaire and Verlaine and the author of some original poems
of great promise. He shot himself at the beginning of his period
of military service. The 'little saviour's burden' is an allusion to
the legend of St Christopher. Written 4–5 November 1908.

From THE DUINO ELEGIES (1923)
Duineser Elegien

The First Elegy
Gaspara Stampa (1523–54), an Italian poetess of noble family
who recorded her at first happy and then unrequited love in
some 200 sonnets. This Elegy was written in January 1912.

The Ninth Elegy
February 1922, except for the first six and the last three lines.

From THE SONNETS TO ORPHEUS (1923): FIRST PART
(2–5 February 1922)
Die Sonette an Orpheus

VII. *'Praising, that's it! As a praiser and a blesser'.* 'Rühmen, das
ists! Ein zum Rühmen Bestellter'

IX. *'Only by him with whose lays'.* 'Nur wer die Leier schon hob'

XXIII. *'Only when flight shall soar'.* 'O erst dann, wenn der Flug

XXVI. *'You that could sound till the end, though, immortal accorder'.*
'Du aber, Göttlicher, du, bis zuletzt noch Ertöner'

From THE SONNETS TO ORPHEUS: SECOND PART
(15–23 February 1922)
Die Sonette an Orpheus

IV. *'This is the creature there has never been'.* 'O dieses ist das
Tier, das es nicht gibt'

X. *'Long will machinery menace the whole of our treasure'.* 'Alles
Erworbne bedroht die Maschine'

XV. *'O fountain mouth, you mouth that can respond'.* 'O Brunnen-
Mund, du gebender, du Mund'

XVII. *'Where, in what ever-blissfully watered gardens, upon what
trees'.* 'Wo, in welchen immer selig bewässerten Gärten'

From THE UNCOLLECTED POEMS OF 1906 TO 1926

The Raising of Lazarus. Auferweckung des Lazarus
Written at Ronda, January 1913.

The Spirit Ariel. Der Geist Ariel
Written at Ronda, early 1913.

Shatter me, music. Bestürz mich, Musik
Paris, May 1913.

Behind the innocent trees. Hinter den schuldlosen Bäumen
Heiligendamm, August 1913.

The Great Night. Die grosse Nacht
Paris, January 1914.

Beloved, lost to begin with. Du im Voraus verlorene Geliebte
Paris, winter 1913–14.

Exposed on the heart's mountains. Ausgesetzt auf den Bergen des
Herzens
Irschenhausen, 20 September 1914.

Time and again. Immer wieder
  Munich, end of 1914.

To Music. An die Musik
  Munich, 11–12 January 1918.

From the Poems of Count C. W. Aus den Gedichten des Grafen
C. W.
  Schloss Berg am Irchel, end of November 1920.

Meaningful word, 'inclination'. Neigung: wahrhaftes Wort!
  Muzot, c. 23 February 1922.

Strongest Star. Starker Stern
  After his health had begun to disintegrate and he had been
compelled to try the first of many increasingly necessary visits
to the sanatorium where, about three years after, he was to die,
Rilke recorded that on the evening of his return to Muzot, in
January 1924, the planet Venus was *'admirablement visible'*.
Written at Muzot, 20 and 22 January 1924.

The Fruit. Die Frucht
  Muzot, late January 1924.

Early Spring. Vorfrühling
  Muzot, mid-February 1924.

Gods, for all we can tell. Götter schreiten vielleicht
  Muzot, late February 1924.

The sap is mounting back. Schon kehrt der Saft aus jener Allge-
meinheit
  Muzot, early March 1924.

On the sunny road. Auf der sonngewohnten Strasse
  Muzot, early June 1924.

The one birds plunge through. Durch den sich Vögel werfen
  Muzot, 16 June 1924.

For Count Karl Lanckoronski. Geschrieben für Karl Grafen
Lanckoronski
  This poem was described by Rilke as an 'improvization' and
inspired by the penultimate line (with which it begins) of a
short poem by Count Lanckoronski, whose poems he had been

reading in manuscript. Written at Ragaz on 10 August 1926, about four months before his death, it is his last great poem and might almost be called his confession of faith.

Epitaph.

Composed before 27 October 1925 and inscribed, according to his wish, on his tombstone in the churchyard at Raron.

READ MORE IN PENGUIN

In every corner of the world, on every subject under the sun, Penguin represents quality and variety – the very best in publishing today.

For complete information about books available from Penguin – including Puffins, Penguin Classics and Arkana – and how to order them, write to us at the appropriate address below. Please note that for copyright reasons the selection of books varies from country to country.

In the United Kingdom: Please write to *Dept. EP, Penguin Books Ltd, Bath Road, Harmondsworth, West Drayton, Middlesex UB7 ODA*

In the United States: Please write to *Consumer Sales, Penguin Putnam Inc., P.O. Box 12289 Dept. B, Newark, New Jersey 07101-5289*. VISA and MasterCard holders call 1-800-788-6262 to order Penguin titles

In Canada: Please write to *Penguin Books Canada Ltd, 10 Alcorn Avenue, Suite 300, Toronto, Ontario M4V 3B2*

In Australia: Please write to *Penguin Books Australia Ltd, P.O. Box 257, Ringwood, Victoria 3134*

In New Zealand: Please write to *Penguin Books (NZ) Ltd, Private Bag 102902, North Shore Mail Centre, Auckland 10*

In India: Please write to *Penguin Books India Pvt Ltd, 11 Community Centre, Panchsheel Park, New Delhi 110017*

In the Netherlands: Please write to *Penguin Books Netherlands bv, Postbus 3507, NL-1001 AH Amsterdam*

In Germany: Please write to *Penguin Books Deutschland GmbH, Metzlerstrasse 26, 60594 Frankfurt am Main*

In Spain: Please write to *Penguin Books S. A., Bravo Murillo 19, 1° B, 28015 Madrid*

In Italy: Please write to *Penguin Italia s.r.l., Via Benedetto Croce 2, 20094 Corsico, Milano*

In France: Please write to *Penguin France, Le Carré Wilson, 62 rue Benjamin Baillaud, 31500 Toulouse*

In Japan: Please write to *Penguin Books Japan Ltd, Kaneko Building, 2-3-25 Koraku, Bunkyo-Ku, Tokyo 112*

In South Africa: Please write to *Penguin Books South Africa (Pty) Ltd, Private Bag X14, Parkview, 2122 Johannesburg*

READ MORE IN PENGUIN

Published or forthcoming:

Swann's Way Marcel Proust

This first book of Proust's supreme masterpiece, *A la recherche du temps perdu*, recalls the early youth of Charles Swann in the small, provincial backwater of Combray through the eyes of the adult narrator. The story then moves forward to Swann's life as a man of fashion in the glittering world of *belle-époque* Paris. A scathing, often comic dissection of French society, *Swann's Way* is also a story of past moments tantalizingly lost and, finally, triumphantly rediscovered.

Metamorphosis and Other Stories Franz Kafka

A companion volume to *The Great Wall of China and Other Short Works*, these translations bring together the small proportion of Kafka's works that he thought worthy of publication. This volume contains his most famous story, 'Metamorphosis'. All the stories reveal the breadth of Kafka's literary vision and the extraordinary imaginative depth of his thought.

Cancer Ward Aleksandr Solzhenitsyn

One of the great allegorical masterpieces of world literature, *Cancer Ward* is both a deeply compassionate study of people facing terminal illness and a brilliant dissection of the 'cancerous' Soviet police state. Withdrawn from publication in Russia in 1964, it became a work that awoke the conscience of the world. 'Without doubt the greatest Russian novelist of this century' *Sunday Times*

Peter Camenzind Hermann Hesse

In a moment of 'emotion recollected in tranquility' Peter Camenzind recounts the days of his youth: his childhood in a remote mountain village, his abiding love of nature, and the discovery of literature which inspires him to leave the village and become a writer. 'One of the most penetrating accounts of a young man trying to discover the nature of his creative talent' *The Times Literary Supplement*